a Year
& other poems

Also by Jos Charles

feeld
Safe Space

a Year
& other poems

Jos Charles

MILKWEED EDITIONS

Published 2022 by Milkweed Editions
Printed in Canada
Cover design by Mary Austin Speaker
Cover art: Alma Woodsey Thomas (1891-1978), *Untitled*, 1960s, watercolor on paper, 9 5/8 x 12 1/8 inches, The Columbus Museum, Georgia; Gift of Miss John Maurice Thomas in memory of her parents John H. and Amelia W. Cantey Thomas and her sister Alma Woodsey Thomas G.1994.20.42

22 23 24 25 26   5 4 3 2 1

First Edition

Library of Congress Cataloging-in-Publication Data

Names: Charles, Jos, 1988- author.
Title: A year : & other poems / by Jos Charles.
Description: First Edition. | Minneapolis, Missesota : Milkweed Editions, 2022. | Summary: "From the celebrated author of feeld comes a formally commanding third collection, dexterously recounting the survival of a period suffused with mourning"—Provided by publisher.
Identifiers: LCCN 2021037275 (print) | LCCN 2021037276 (ebook) | ISBN 9781571315472 (hardback) | ISBN 9781571317667 (ebook)
Subjects: LCGFT: Poetry.
Classification: LCC PS3603.H37647 Y43 2022 (print) | LCC PS3603. H37647 (ebook) | DDC 813/.6--dc23
LC record available at https://lccn.loc.gov/2021037275
LC ebook record available at https://lccn.loc.gov/2021037276

Milkweed Editions is committed to ecological stewardship. We strive to align our book production practices with this principle, and to reduce the impact of our operations in the environment. We are a member of the Green Press Initiative, a nonprofit coalition of publishers, manufacturers, and authors working to protect the world's endangered forests and conserve natural resources. *a Year* was printed on acid-free 100% postconsumer-waste paper by Friesens Corporation.

CONTENTS

for the lost—

a Year
& other poems

LIKE YOU

I looked for arbors to bend beneath carried circuits

countless in the blood myself from room

to room to see a city

square pin calendars to walls

& hear, I have heard, of inventories of

names dead unspoken

as if the first

I'D CLIMB TO SEE

but having climbed a little on
you reached a mountain cut out the sky

To say nothing of before how
words might sculpt sculpt midair

When I'd heard rustling I inched
slower down the colder mountainside

WHERE out from under story or

carriage pooled to the floor it's pressed to

new growth a mushroom up from bathroom tiles

of a house where xmas lights loom still togethered a yoke

of violet overhead & it could not matter less if you look

where up from floors restingless plotless shelterless green

a Year

January

Desert hills all
aflame The old hopes
        an oak shook through a screen

Our separate smoke
caught
        in the same ascent Months
        I move in you

Rosemary
dead Naomi at the clinic
        Leah in hospice in bed
        & debt Throwing a book
        to the thresher a poet read
        So much less than our
        nakedness   a chorus
                        a garland
                        of changing names

Awaiting
not clarity
but mineral a membrane
                    between us stooping
                    to rock a woman rises
                    armful of color of
                    evening
                    kelp

A current
gives as much as it has

given you who I
I swear saw

gone round the tidepools yesterday at noon But the world is
gone But the world is

a lake the shape of
a lake

Awaiting not clarity but the shadow of something clear

All night a hormone I pant It is not for wont of

understanding I place notes to turn to after this

February

Walked
aenigma of
aenigma past each house
             Saw a crow pick its
             earth the only earth
A man's hand unasks my back
             Heard a pool deflate
             Monday you would be
                       twenty-eight Open

             door electric fan in it

Hole as
expanse of breath of
      leaven as knife
      to dough &
      downed the book
store neighborhood &
those quote rough streets clerk
says past eighth
                  street
lights sudden coming on

We drink our
mouths a
blue with blood
I can't Wearing a star
        she wrote
        what is needed is
        a history of
        mouths
Already noon over
filled   with houseplants

Weight
　　　hour on
　　　hour holding in

a café broke
　　　the car meds writing
　　　on napkins lunchbreak when
　　　ever it was I read I
　　　　　　　long so
　　　much for my beloved dead
　　　ones The day of miracle being
　　　past The day a plot a grove
we make & know which breath held time

In desert
clouds draw earth

You point a hand A flood could happen
there We walk all day to
                    jobs shops Say words refer to
                    what isn't there From bed that night

                    rain two horn of ram mesquite trees
                    said afterlife

March

Busied my
self with days
　　　　leaflets
　　　　breathless days
　　　　of belief or
　　　　wanting belief
Inscriptions of the coming
heart　　　when boys
　　　　would hold your
　　　　comprehensible
　　　　neck & place boy
　　　　you were so much to be free

The ceilings
I went under Dandelion
stuffed in pocket & what was it dogwood
        Mother stood coordinated
        lemons his hair a molest
        of vellum I bathed

understood unbelievable each emblem Signifier

        me Asleep
        in rooms I still sleep

Tuesday first time I saw deer a corpse of rot orange burnt amberous
of inside leaping under I saw thru canopies of collapsing light

The hour has an understory
I was a child pulling grass in the understory
                dissembling until we met When I'd
                pull branch to ledge & sing all
                        afternoon one song
                        atop another

I had not
begun to think past
testament of want
      I didn't want
      I believed sentences knew their end
      I wore bathing suits still on the porch of world
         I had not begun to answer
         what is the same (it
is your mouth only that has changed)
         Joshua oh
         Joshua
         oh

April

I put you into a poem
You climbed the giantest tree

I put a dozen grapefruit into a tree
You ate every one There is a letter

in a desk I cannot know
One day I will

Walked
slower each week
I write
of the city Women
        weep here for
        dogs

        they speak too

We speak
a language capable of itself
                  only it is
                  true the outside an
                  organ

                  your eye

                  on a platter
of silver & laurel

        the city around us fallen
        daily the news Rome has fallen

The river is cold
The poem is perhaps

a room

a charwoman
at its feet Under the blue blue sky

It is Wednesday Dead things

sink in the sky alive

If I have misspoke let me
be clear There is one who sleeps at night one
                who is the leopard at your feet (you
                who are a leopard) another outfitted
                        passes another in silence

May

You see what no one
sees
hair cedar on a shore your
hair galleries of feather by
feather
the sun

Having fled the garden the inevitable

envelopes

you Marie clung
a colt to the other side of a fence   In you
    anthologies

    of meadow clinging

Gone mad for weeks I linger 110 degrees & who

would dare to leave a room Tops flood the floor green

Awake absenting the here I make   A man asks me to feint

Asked to eat a peach on screen I write for days my love

is like a raven o'er the flood (& there is never not a flood)

(balms in heads of honeycomb) (an architect in every room)

A book
is a margin I go
to put holly to the lip A proximity
to what one is not
to bury yourself
to
what morrow
allows Not sorrow
Everything against it

You
touch long
irretrievable
beside you again
me again
in the dark of our certainty
I hold like a stone &
even you I turn
my head to a thousand possible things
gone It is all I hold
now & spring

June

A woman
cradles
nothing in
her arms
  welcome
    exists here
    too beech
    wood

Exists
in any
condition
seed a bone
calcified to style like
the limes you left becoming fact like health is
                            institutional how yellow
                            might be spread
                            printed
floral folded on a shelf

These
considerations are
a question of fit who or
                    ought the task the same

                    to be of use
                    in this

                    city you
                    show

me where the limit
begins reminded of proportion
                    the politics of proportion

I wanted to believe
a corner a print leaned to
a corner can save
a people   The revolution to
                 each stagnancy
                 my romancing
        the condo on the block
                 placing only
                 the limit of
                 its form

                 Questions
        within the body you forget
                 breaks holding
                 breaks
                 in
                 the wall

Unsettled
day I cannot contain
more than myself my belongings historic boxes
spread the street blue a fume of
doves
above it
& thought
of one I love

July

        Slept in cars
    sheave of hair shook
    in rain California
    a fire my mind
    entirely   a house of cinder in
                   a house of cinder
        Iterable rows months mast
in the anywhere Shoulder me there

A scandal
       three cartons red
       in a hedge
       in
each the thousand eye research of flies

Flags ask
out pride winds
from the terrace
interview at six
interview at eight
a woman waiting unholds your form a man's bathroom
I'm always in
empty summer
homes by the sea

These workless days
                   a fit foam
                   the corner of my mouth
on a floor Partita Thursday My heart
                   as big as it is over
                   a toilette forgetting that Bachmann
                   poem you love
                   Let's swap our shirts
                   Let us hold a coconut It is dusk

Have you seen
town from a hill

a hill from town
all downed in wire woe

A ground floor
where nobody lives

    & like a scabbard we shuffle through

August

Late I walk through you Mistook
                people a partly worn port

Thought the same thought Martin
                killing Paul No tide tonight dry
                speechless weeds in the brush

About a pigeon corpse gulls We threw
                our baubles to the sea

Remembered birch in the drift
of where you worked Forgot my coat
backpack
phone   Purlieus
                              of stone scuttle in the sticks
                              of throat Medallions
          again in the birch Earth
          calendric ready to close
          heedable in
                              ahead
          dammed your hand living
          through it Finchwing
          eavesdropped to this

Nonetheless I have my nest
my two blue wrists suggesting
warmth Beside a row of
        hyacinths cold a poet

        wakes to the thicket she sleeps

(5 am a meridian
a cathexis

        deer cart
        oranges through the air)

Closing time foolish plays above a butcher's block
It is not easy Black line on a street from a flag
of blue & black I have accepted walking past

the too lit district to get to you Under the logic
of cloud the logic of a window shade I live on
where the mulberry bleeds where they bury

I have accepted this cisterns underground
If a door does not suffice they build
corridors lower it is not easy you Asterion

September

A house
under construction

faded fence a pear
rot in sun

who knew
measurement
a parliament of lamps where a light dims
a window left open
enough for you
to appear

It is not
enough
One wind on
a microphone
Out
line of a figure of
a bruise

Remembered
september or
november Any
month the same really
Like working the street
a bar free drinks from
creeps at the bar
Together a laugh
lodged in air Taste
of blood copper
rain This
existence
sister a theft
The Friday you left
the rain picking up
hasn't been the same

A berry fallen
from a crown of
goathorn broke
entirely from
the sheet of
fur you lifted
me from while
wind blew continuous
shut the door

With grace
I am with you
in your labor until
    the last & I am
    joyful today for
    its structure Machinery clips the makers hand

    Impossible the leaves have changed

October

October rose
up A coastline obstructing
        itself I
        lost something
        in every room they
got in how
            how
            how
            how your dreams

When was it
I knew my house to be
     falling apart
     when did I lift
     an arm or bend
     backward corbel like swung you your back
     to mine When was it ever September tides pouring over
When whales like men moved about the earth

Walked home
from the pharmacy
looked in bushes backs
of birds heard a ring (every
ring is a dead ring) & were you alive
last it rained when two
                sisters ahead la la
                they said if we could
                la no
        femme flaneur my brain la
        a living horse wooden
        soldiers in it

Perpetual hair falls
to the floor Harpies make a nest there

No book whose margin isn't illumined
with carmine carbon gold

When you get back
they will say

we tore down a house & built a statue of a house

I see you
at night Our
brief

        kind an
        oak signifies
        Goethe like becomes its arm
We peek then ate
We the fruit

November

I press each leaf

(the unfaceable too into your leaves)

Pigment presses out
you in
you
laurel
not yet in the wind

All Saturday a fire
Household downed
in bustling Ceasefirelessly leaf
approaches leaf I built
exits Canopies to come
back to World
welted I lean in

                    The air
                  winter
color national in its mass like
            wool & there are
            those who sort wool
            & it is work to bow to fold a hand
            upon a hand Election day
            interred sheltered
            the wood us

Water floods
beneath us chambers of water beneath

Visible even the unseen

Overcast & fielding our street you were

No new word
having fed every

      word being only one
      word
        Ram

      Her two eyes in the leaves

December

All that turns
is a wheel The sky
is ashen & a wheel that is turning as we cross
a bridge of stone

It is not yet noon in the port
where I live Like any a poem
that is after you Paul at Pont Mirabeau

We touch a bridge & therefore its stone
To touch a stone is forever to touch a bridge

In the street
they are starting fires It warms even us

What was crossed out is not the same
as what was never written down

Mountains mind even us

Looked at last at the branch that
                    plaits your face Symptom
                    like we cling gardener to each

Love referentless

From the roof of
the apartment branches break their pits seedless

                    within it men in
                    trees sing

In the aenigma
of a shadow

of a window left open
for wind
to leave In the thought

that cannot account for form & having spent

thought
we encounter form only In the distance

between the hole of
a stone & a dove within it

Of all we have

imagined & we have
imagined such distances What is known

& not known You touch
the stone it could be any

stone I live on

It is falling
ash in Santa Ana falling in your year
                              irrecoverably
                              in the evening
                  holding hands our
                              selves
                              into the evening
                                    we wept a
                                    quiet English
                              the day contained

(Such silence sudden
now in the clearing A tarp
chains the lot of our speech
                    Sunday   no women washing at the washing
                                stones The past is only
                                the only mutable thing)

                                A lone tanker
                                in the waves swims

102

& other poems

A NOTE *on language*

Never having lived
among but beside form
I no longer look where
the city lifts a little further
past houses, ocean, light
from a crane no longer
looking the child hurried
beside a mother moving
too too fast at what escapes
the grasp of leaves & awnings
of leaves, past what is lifted
whatever word from
whatever throat it's lodged
there being only one throat
between us, past perception
& nevertheless perceiving
as we must what moves between
us, no longer roof but atmosphere
precursor & remnant of speech
remaining as it must perhaps
the least effective of our music

A NEW YORK POEM

A brain is like the heart but stupid we text
    in a subway corridor no service salt hair pollenate
    ash exiting exhausted sneezing
    blood through a park

A man quotes the Raven beside & we do
    not dare mention equivalence summer grass from lawns torn dollars
    in the hands of children clinging to roots only to pass
    time exhausted as the world heaves

A crow at our feet in daylight as we—no
    not discover anything but discover—between us
    gliding flockless a raven
    a raven & a crow & a raven

A FANTASY

Undiagnosable the concurrence of a squirrel
as I grope the branch it climbs & carrying an umbrella as I was
& spilling my eyes not interruption but the logic of concert
& lost the line given as I am to misfiring running
thru shrubs mushrooms in roots almost screaming
it seems so little to matter this morning in a room
within a room in a country given to misfiring
& losing as it does not only words & climbing
the largest oak at school I remember
back pack on my back full of rocks
& smelling as I did unlike I should
& not speaking as I do & no one
would kick so high I thought of
Zacchaeus when they took me
down groping at spilling rock
& almost awake out a dream
today I turn to you to say
I think I will go running

A SONG

Putting my finger through
the hole the finch climbed through

                a man, the very hose in his hand—
                a fruit carton props the door

        There is no question of before
        Only pathless when you walk before
        Or I walk before Meadowlike

        Godshadow
        What we show of it

A LYRIC

Preservation merely is compost
delayed A jug burst to ground

any ground & whose & after all we put
into a mouth we speak nearly of truth

what waits to be said & giving I said
to a room of any but you, if I have spoken

of trees I merely & only have meant
the gracious indifference of trees

A NOTE *on form*

Do not die, they say
at least today, full of sense
the pocket of city-planted shrubs
lining the street not built they say
but given Concrete, the paint bucket of
a man spilling dashed lines to road It is sense
he makes & the brushfire from hills, these
too are desert hills, spills to the road where
we do not speak of poetry, a bridge built
to burn itself, not unlike a mind So open fire
already open the fire boundless & stoking
I do not know what else there is at times, narrative
material split from raw material or preserving
the split only to talk on a mezzanine later
of men the wood we live & under a star
of branch the unsayable possible in line
to say this was our desire

Acknowledgments

A number of the poems herein are written for others—the work of others, conversations shared, odes to friends, elegies.

While not exhaustive, those below mark an occasion of composition that was explicit to me, one which I owe endless thanks. I write after you.

'A current' & 'All that turns' are after Paul Celan
        (p12, p97).
'Hole as' is after George C. (p18).
'We drink our' is after Carolyn Charles (p19).
'Weight' is after Nelly Sachs (p20).
'The hour too has an understory' is after manuel arturo
        abreu (p28).
'The river is cold' is after Fady Joudah (p36).
'Having fled the garden the inevitable' is after B.
        (p42).
'Gone mad for weeks I linger' is after Harryette
        Mullen (p43).
'A book is a margin' is after Kaveh Akbar (p44).
'These workless days' is after Hoa Nguyen (p60).
'Late I walk through you' & 'Remembered birch in the
        drift' are after Taneum Bambrick (p65, p66).
'Closing time foolish' is after Spencer Krug (p69).
'Remember 2014' is after B.A. (p75).

'Water floods' is after Russell Atkins (p92).
'In the aenigma' is after Éduoard Glissant (p99).
'It is falling' is after Ariana Reines (p101).
'A New York Poem' is after Chase Berggrun (p104).

To the writers who followed, supported, struggled with, & bettered *a Year & other poems* through its drafts: manuel arturo abreu, Kaveh Akbar, Taneum Bambrick, Chase Berggrun, Ilya Kaminsky, Rickey Laurentiis, Loma, Aditi Machado, Farid Matuk, Claire Schwartz, Solmaz Sharif; to my comrades & friends who watched, tended, & fought throughout the writing; to Carolyn; to Bernadette; to j.c.; to the National Bail Out collective; to Milkweed & everyone involved in the production, circulation, & reception of *a Year & other poems*; to those who persist—out of possibility, necessity, for the sake of another.

Sergio De La Torre

Jos Charles is the author of *feeld*, a Pulitzer-finalist and winner of the 2017 National Poetry Series selected by Fady Joudah, and *Safe Space*. In 2016 she received the Ruth Lilly and Dorothy Sargent Rosenberg Fellowship through the Poetry Foundation. Jos Charles has an MFA from the University of Arizona. She is a PhD student at the University of California Irvine and currently resides in Long Beach, California.

milkweed
editions

Founded as a nonprofit organization in 1980, Milkweed Editions
is an independent publisher. Our mission is to identify, nurture
and publish transformative literature, and build an engaged
community around it.

Milkweed Editions is based in Bdé Óta Othúŋwe (Minneapolis)
within Mní Sota Makhóčhe, the traditional homeland of
the Dakhóta people. Residing here since time immemorial,
Dakhóta people still call Mní Sota Makhóčhe home, with four
federally recognized Dakhóta nations and many more Dakhóta
people residing in what is now the state of Minnesota. Due to
continued legacies of colonization, genocide, and forced removal,
generations of Dakhóta people remain disenfranchised from their
traditional homeland. Presently, Mní Sota Makhóčhe has become
a refuge and home for many Indigenous nations and peoples,
including seven federally recognized Ojibwe nations. We humbly
encourage our readers to reflect upon the historical legacies held
in the lands they occupy.

milkweed.org

Milkweed Editions, an independent nonprofit publisher, gratefully acknowledges sustaining support from our Board of Directors; the Alan B. Slifka Foundation and its president, Riva Ariella Ritvo-Slifka; the Amazon Literary Partnership; the Ballard Spahr Foundation; *Copper Nickel*; the McKnight Foundation; the National Endowment for the Arts; the National Poetry Series; the Target Foundation; and other generous contributions from foundations, corporations, and individuals. Also, this activity is made possible by the voters of Minnesota through a Minnesota State Arts Board Operating Support grant, thanks to a legislative appropriation from the arts and cultural heritage fund. For a full listing of Milkweed Editions supporters, please visit milkweed.org.

A portion of the proceeds generated by this publication will be shared by the author and publisher with the National Bail Out Collective, which supports ongoing bail reform efforts and creates resources for organizers and advocates interested in ending pretrial detention. For more information on the NBO, please visit their website at www.nationalbailout.org.

Interior design by Tijqua Daiker
Typeset in Bell MT

Bell was designed by Richard Austin in 1788 for the British Letter Foundry. Bell has a number of elaborate details reminiscent of the steely calligraphy of the period. It was influenced by the radical Didone styles of type, however Bell is less severe than the French models and is now classified as Transitional. This typeface became popular in the United States in the early twentieth century with artisan printers.